Is that Spaghetti on the Ceiling?

MOMENTS OF MOTHERHOOD & MAYHEM IN VERSE

THE AUTHOR Judy Rose was born in London in 1956. She started writing poems in 1993 and in 1995 read them every fortnight on BBC Radio Gloucestershire. Since the publication of her first book, *Fridge over Troubled Water,* many of her poems have been heard on national radio and television. She is currently the resident poet for BBC Radio Devon and also has a regular column in *Devon Today.* She has taken her Poetry Performance 'A Day in the Life of a Forty Something' to many parts of the country. She lives in Devon where she and her husband farm llamas. They have two sons.

To my sisters Brynna and Leanda, with love

Also by Judy Rose

Fridge over Troubled Water
Mummy said the 'B' Word

Is that Spaghetti on the Ceiling?

MOMENTS OF MOTHERHOOD & MAYHEM IN VERSE

JUDY ROSE

THE WINDRUSH PRESS · GLOUCESTERSHIRE

First published in Great Britain by
The Windrush Press in 2000
Little Window, High Street,
Moreton-in-Marsh
Gloucestershire GL56 OLL

Tel: 01608 652012
Fax: 01608 652125
Email: Windrush@windrushpress.com
Website: www.windrushpress.com

British Library in Cataloguing Data
A catalogue record for this book is available from the British Library

ISBN 1 900624 42 7

Typeset by Archetype IT Ltd, website www.archetype-it.com
Printed and bound in Great Britain by Biddles Ltd, Guildford

Cover design by Mark-making Design
Front cover photograph © Tony Stone Images / Donna Day

Contents

Those Joys of Motherhood

Girl Talk

In Holiday Mood

Home Sweet Home

Growing Old Disgracefully

Those Joys of Motherhood

Is that Spaghetti on the Ceiling?
(or *Once Upon a Slime*)

Children eating Spaghetti; it's not a pretty sight.
I've yet to meet a single child who has learnt to do it right.
Is it a well kept secret, that no child ever knows?
You put it in your mouth, not down your neck or up your nose!

Some just pretend they are eating worms, they love a spot of slime,
They pucker lips and cross their eyes, suck one strand at a time.
And others simply shovel it from plate to mouth and hair
And only pause when desperate to come up for some air!

And what about the sound effects? The sucking and the slurping
The smacking of those orange lips as well as noisy burping.
But there's a silent menace; you will not hear a sound
For spaghetti is so quiet as it slithers to the ground.

Beware spaghetti aftermath; don't be surprised at all
At far flung pasta clinging to the ceiling or the wall.
Yes, children eating spaghetti...the horror of it lingers...
So these days, when it comes to lunch,
They will probably get
Fish Fingers!

Morning has Broken

I'm woken by the smoke alarm
At six. With mounting dread
I rush down to the kitchen
Kids yell, 'Go back to bed.'

I strain to hear toast being scraped
And noisy whispering;
'Put thick jam on the burnt bits
She'll never guess a thing.'

An incident upon the stairs!
A breakage has occurred.
Then follow some expletives
I'd rather not have heard.

Angelic offspring enter
One yielding laden tray.
While gorgeous hand-picked flowers
Are being thrust my way.

Since weeds are all we seem to grow
It's fairly safe to say
Our neighbour has, unwittingly
Supplied *The Big Bouquet.*

My look of pleasure-tinged-with-angst
Betrays my sense of woe,
'It's okay mum, we picked them
From a place it wouldn't show.'

They're sure that she won't notice
I inwardly demur;
Alas there'll be no prizes
For her dahlias this year.

Compared to what is coming next
This incident is minor,
They've pulled out all the stops today
And gone for antique china.

The only heirloom I possess
Now lurches into view
'I climbed a chair to get to it...
I nearly dropped it too.'

With huge relief take hold of cup
And gulp the tepid tea
The *extra* sugar in it
Being quite a novelty.

'What, all those cocoa pops for me?
Ooh yummy, how fantastic.'
The toast is quite a challenge
Hope I look enthusiastic.

I read their precious home made cards
And wipe my tears away.
High drama, secrets, spills and thrills;
It must be
Mother's Day.

The Hoarse Whisperer

Children's outing to the pictures
Is not such a happy lot
When a member in the party
Has severely lost the plot.

In a very noisy whisper
His confusion is expressed;
Quick and quiet explanation
Is the mother's urgent quest.

You, of course, must keep your voice down
Yet ensure that you are heard.
'I can't hear you mummy! LOUDER!'
Those around us get perturbed.

Why is Pocahontas crying?
Is poor Bambi's mummy dead?
Is the Lion King a baddie?
Who kicked Woody off the bed?

Why are dinosaurs so hungry?
Why is Hercules so tough?
(*Why are you eating all my popcorn?*
STOP IT MUM! YOU'VE HAD ENOUGH!)

What's a hunchback? Does it hurt much?
Did Aladdin steal that lamp?
Why are those Dalmatians spotty?
Which one's Lady, which one's Tramp?

By the time the question's answered
To your offspring's satisfaction,
You have missed at least ten minutes
And the next twist in the action.

Running commentaries given;
Has he grasped the point at last?
Frankly kids' films have a drawback ...
Their plots thicken far too fast.

It's in his Kiss

This toddler's mum is going out
And dressed up ultra smart.
But there is a dilemma
When mum and son must part.

My timing is not good at all;
He's half way through his tea!
The face that lunched a thousand chips
Is bearing down on me.

Of course I want to say goodbye
And share a warm embrace
Just one thing now deters me;
The meal around his face!

And then those sticky fingers,
I cannot help but wince
When thinking of my linen suit
Plus greasy fingerprints.

I can't resist those outstretched arms,
That loving invitation;
I quickly snatch a tea-cloth
For some damage limitation.

But sadly, it's to no avail
For HE casts it asunder!
(Was this a dry-clean only suit?
I cannot help but wonder.)

And as I feel two sticky hands
Clasped round me very tight
I ponder on the wisdom
Of mothers who wear WHITE!

Yet happily I leave my son
Sustained by the belief
I may well start a fashion trend
With my *ketchup-print* motif!

Let's Stick Together

A very cosy scene indeed
The toddler and his mum
All set to make a collage;
(*Blue Peter type of fun*).

But only fifteen seconds in
Of cutting out and glueing,
The mother's instinct tells her
That there is trouble brewing.

He's squeezing out the tube of glue
As hard as he is able;
It squelches quite dramatically
Across the dining table.

'We only glue on paper, RIGHT!'
The poor mite looks admonished.
'We NEVER glue on tables
That we've just had French-polished.'

He scoops the glue up with his hands
'NO, DON'T DO THAT!' shrieks mummy.
And in a flash he's wiped the lot
All down his chest and tummy.

She quickly claps his little hand
This was not very clever,
For as the glue is hardening
She notes they're stuck together.

'Oh why did I use super glue?'
She cries, now quite demented
As – though not quite as she had hoped –
Their bond is well cemented.

Name Tape Blues

I've bought my son's school uniform
Long day. Huge cost. PLUS FIGHTS.
Son deeply miffed
Re footwear rift;
Mum cannot run to Nikes.

You'd think the hard part's over
But worse is yet to come;
A task to make
Eyes cross, neck ache
Not to mention fingers numb.

For strewn across the sofa, floor
Piled up on every table
Are endless bits
Of new school kit
All needing a named label.

The task seems insurmountable
I swoon, come over feeble.
For I confess
I don't possess
A great way with a needle.

I've simply got to grasp my tool
And do the deed so dreaded.
I rant and rage;
It takes an age
To get said damned tool threaded.

Hours later, fingers very sore
I think I'll pause, take stock.
Am most aggrieved
At what's achieved;
Two shirts and one rugby sock!

Pricked fingers have caused bloodshed
I hope the red won't show.
I sigh and frown
Three garments down
And forty-six to go.

I wish I'd started earlier
Spread out this endless toil.
'THREE PAIRS OF PANTS!?'
The mother rants
As she burns the midnight oil.

Amidst the navy, white and grey
Of shirts, socks, shorts and shoes,
I'm just another
Hapless mother
In the grip of name tape blues.

This dreary task comes round each year
It is our fate...remember
There's no escape
Till you've got it taped...
In the first week of September.

It Won't be all White on the Night

With mounting trepidation
I open son's kit bag
And extricate what seems to be
A filthy, screwed-up rag.

But then on close inspection
Through the well-embedded dirt
I recognise, with sinking heart
And dread... *a football shirt!*

And this is how it always starts
The long and painful story
Of restoring 'gruesome garment'
To its former white-ish glory.

I often ask the question
As I scrub with all my might
Who was it, in their wisdom
Went and chose the colour WHITE?

For white shows stubborn stains
That even Persil mums can't banish
(Despite a brave pre-wash attack
With a little bar of Vanish.)

For we are talking MUD
That bio enzymes cannot reach
(Despite long soak in every single
Bloody brand of bleach.)

Whoever made this colour choice
Deserves a bit of flack...
You could have made lives easier
If you'd only gone for BLACK!

So spare a thought for all of us
Immersed in Kit-Bag glums
Next time you choose new football shirts
Do please consult the Mums!

Getting to Gnaw You

The theory: teach kids nurture skills
At young and tender age.
Reluctantly buy rodent
In strong escape-proof cage.

I vowed it would not get to me
That I would not be beat
And then I felt a fluffiness
(Vicinity of feet!)

I chant 'It's just a mouse'
Which just exacerbates my fear.
I scream. I mount the nearest chair.
I swing from chandelier.

The children now rush to the scene
And sense things have got tricky,
Their sympathy alas misplaced;
'*You're frightening poor Mickey*'.

Though glad that 'nurture skills' have grown
Must issue heartfelt plea;
'I'm sorry one of us must go
It's either him or me.'

My offspring ponder this awhile
Conferring with each other.
Pride stops me telling you their choice...
Let's just say it's not MOTHER!!!

Girl Talk

Brawn Free

I've tried to stretch, I've stepped, I've even burned
As seen on all those work-out videos
And in this quest I've left no limb unturned.
(Nor tendon, muscle, joint un-pulled God knows)
I've tried to shape up Cindy Crawford's way.
I've tried to copy Claudia and Cher,
But working out with babes I have to say
Just lowers self-esteem, brings on despair.
From all this pain and cost I had expected
A firm and lissom me would soon be born,
But sadly, no great change can be detected
(Unless you count all bruised and overdrawn.)
Though sightings of my bulges leave me squirming
I must conclude; *The lady's not for firming!*

Short Straw Strop

I'm in the bank and stuck behind
The one you love to hate;
She's banking all the takings
From the local Summer Fête.
She wants to do a recount on
Three thousand five pence pieces!
Oooh great; I've time to knit a scarf
And write a lengthy thesis!

At M and S, a stressful scene
That's difficult to beat;
A woman's brought back half the shop
But sadly...no receipt!
She has an explanation;
The sales staff can't be kinder.
(Guess who's parked on a yellow line
And in a sweat behind her?)

And at the supermarket
I'm now in 'manic-mode'
For her-in-front has items
Which alas, have no bar code!
At last, it's my turn to be served
But feel my life-blood draining;
'This till is closing down now
For in-house staff retraining!'

And next, the make-up counter.
Ah yes, I might have guessed;
I'm next behind a woman
Undergoing skin-type tests.
She's new to this and needs advice,
The sales girl cannot rush her.
And me? I'm crimson now...with rage;
At least I won't need BLUSHER!

Then driving home I'm following
A type I've met before,
She *thinks* she wants to overtake
But isn't really sure.
And every time I make a move
She veers into my path
She's sailing very close indeed
To road rage aftermath.

These things are sent to try us
And make us loose our cool.
'Just do not let them get to you'
Should be our golden rule.
But someone pulls the shortest straw
And here's the mystery
Can someone, somehow please explain...
Why is it always ME?

The Way You Do

You polished off the children's tea
(The way you always do)
The half fish finger, clammy chips
The stone cold cabbage too.
You've really got no option
You cannot bear the waste;
So finish the fudge yoghurt
Although you hate the taste!

That's how you broke your diet
(The way you always do)
Although you're only on Day One
'Oh well,' you sigh, 'What's new?'
You're angry though for you'd been 'good'
All day...till five-fifteen.
But tea is such a testing time
For food!
Know what I mean?

And then you think, 'Oh what the hell!'
(The way you always do)
Seek out the milk digestives
But just eat one or two.
By then of course you realise
The harm's done anyway;
And so you really go for it....
Eight fun-size Milky Way!

You feel weak-willed and rather sick
(The way you always do)
And then you feel your great resolve
Return to you anew.
You tell yourself, *'Next time I know
I'll see this diet through!'*
And strangely, you believe you will
The way you always do!

Out Damned Spot

First wearing of my brand new blouse
And lo! The greasy stain.
What miracle
Can I perform
To make it clean again?

I'll find some bio-enzymes
That eat up grease and dirt.
Yes, wretched stain,
You'll rue the day
You landed on this shirt.

But wretched stain, you have turned out
More stubborn than you seem
But I am damned
If I am off
To fork out for 'dry clean'.

You really think you've made your mark
But I've met your type before,
When you think I've scrubbed you
All I've got
I'm going to scrub you
A little bit more.

Postscript

Attack on greasy stain proceeds
I scrub with heart and soul
And finally where that stain was
There's now
A little hole.

Choc Absorber

This diet lark too long has been endured;
Two weeks, three days, four hours of self-denial.
And what I really need to take on board
Is, deep down, self control is not my style.
I've had it up to here, with strong will-power
And abstinence from chocolate must now cease.
I must have something *naughty* to devour
Sod outer flab and give me *inner* peace!
To those who always say 'you're what you eat'
I'd sooner be a Mars Bar than Ryvita,
Yes folks, this diet's ended in defeat
The way ahead for me is 'Happy Eater'
Now from my secret cache, the Milk Tray Beckons...
It's 0–60 chocs...in fifteen seconds!

Bag Lady

I'm queuing at the check-out tills
I start to sweat and curse
I've made a grim discovery...
I cannot find my purse.

With trembling hand and heavy heart
I rummage frantically
The contents of my bag pulled out
For one and all to see.

I squirm within as I turn out
Some very fluffy sweets
A lot of Kit-Kat wrappers
And three years' worth of receipts.

And next a gruesome hanky
Left festering too long
(*Was that a gasp of horror*
From the now assembled throng?)

Is this as bad as it can get?
Oh no, friends, not by far;
My diary is welded to
A melting chocolate bar.

And now my hands have gone all blue!
I feel my spirits sink;
To add to woes of missing purse
My biro's leaking ink!

More helpful people gather round
I'm sure they all mean well
As they take in the contents of
The handbag out of hell.

One thinks perhaps I dropped it
One thinks it's left at home.
*(No doubt they all have theories on my
Unappealing comb.)*

I find more Kit-Kat wrappers
My secrets out. I blush.
'That's eight now' says one woman
In the long ensuing hush.

I shake the damned bag upside down
An act of wanton folly;
I've shelled a load of tampons
Into her-behind-me's trolley.

Then hope and pride now all but lost
I find to my surprise
My purse! It's been there all along
Twixt my yoghurts and french fries.

No Pain... No Gain
(or *You Take My Breath Away*)

From personal experience
I've found a major hurdle
In trying to get myself inside
A stomach-firming girdle.
Is there a knack I've somehow missed?
Is there a special skill?
The government should warn us:
'Tummy-toning garments kill.'

They look quite harmless, truth to tell
But do not be mis-led,
While redefining your old shape
They'll leave you...well...half dead!
They do not have a lot of 'give'
So what you must expect
Is an innards-crushing feeling
Plus bulldozer-type effect.

But don't give up! Ignore the pain,
The sweat, your bright red hue,
(The latter, girls, will not last long
For soon you'll go all blue!)
Yes breathing, talking, moving,
Are hard...but you'll be cheered
When you turn sideways and you find
You've almost disappeared!

Scales of Injustice

A four-course meal
With no holds barred.
Next day
The scales.
I dread them.

It took three hours
To gain three pounds,
It will take
Three weeks
To shed them.

If the Cap Fits

Indelicate though it may be
And sorry though I am
I think that *someone* must speak out
About the diaphragm!

You coat the thing with slimy gel
And get a grip...at last,
But cap, with ideas of its own
Just springs straight from your grasp.

It ricochets behind the loo
And lands in fluff and dust.
(You note slight loss of *mellow mood*
And dissipating lust!)

Re-washed and gelled, you persevere
For optimism lingers
But cap (and hopes of passion)
Just slip right through your fingers.

You're angry now, yet don't give up.
Alas your next attempt
Sees cap land in your potted plant
And your libido spent!

And just as with a parking space
You know it's time to say;
'If you fail after three attempts...
You should call it a day!'

You stand there, cap in hand. You curse!
Yes, someone should be blamed
For marketing a product
That simply can't be tamed.

Returning to your partner's snores
You now admit defeat;
Yes, when it comes to birth control
The cap just can't be beat!

In Holiday Mood

First Things First

In two weeks I'll be far away
And lazing in the sun,
But first...an endless list of tasks
Is waiting to be done.

For first...I need new summer clothes
Kit out the kids as well,
They've grown right out of last year's things
(Like mother, truth to tell!)

I've got to stock the first-aid kit
Buy all the sun tan lotions
The anti travel-sickness pills,
Insect-repelling potions.

I've got to order travellers cheques
And foreign currency,
And dig out all the passports
For him and them and me.

Who cares! I'll soon be languishing
Upon a poolside chair
Immersed in Jilly Cooper,
Without a single care...

But first...I've got to organise
The feeding of the pets,
The intricate instructions,
Phone numbers of the vets.

Then stop the milk and papers
And then try to ensure,
That Yellow Pages don't get left
For TWO WEEKS by front door!

Then ask my neighbours *not* to do
What they all did last time,
Which was *ignore* the burglar alarm
And not dial 999!

But really there's no hassle?
I've got it all in hand,
And there'll be no more worries
When I'm laid out on that sand!

But first... The body overhaul
Help! Where should I begin?
I badly need to wax those legs,
Exfoliate my skin.

I'm desperate for a haircut
And of course a pedicure.
A facial wouldn't go amiss
(Though *face-lift might help more!*)

My tummy could do with a 'tuck'
And cellulite is rife,
My breasts, once pert, now badly
Need to get themselves a life!

But damn it all! Why worry?
I'm going to have a ball,
Bikini clad for two whole weeks
A tan will fix it all!

But first...try that bikini on
Make sure I look okay;
One glance confirms the garment
And the body's had their day!

I need to tone those muscles
And lose at least two stone...

...They're overrated, holidays.
I think I'll stay at home!

Packing it In

Think I've finished all my packing
For my two weeks by the sea
Yet I'm feeling rather anxious;
Deep down, something worries me.

Glance at three huge bulging cases
But as every woman knows
There is nothing worse than finding
You've packed insufficient clothes.

What if evenings aren't that balmy?
What if weather isn't good?
Better pack some thermal undies
(And my coat with fur-lined hood.)

Then remember! LYCRA BODY!
Vital for the discothèque
(Yes it does impede my breathing
Quite a lot... but what the heck!)

And supposing Crete's not ready
For yours truly in a thong?
Better pack more 'modest' beachwear
Plus my crab-motif sarong.

Think again about the night life.
What if there's a formal Do?
Hell, I've only packed one ballgown
Need a choice. I'll make that two.

Then a brainwave, pack my trainers!
Good for scrambling on the rocks
In a frenzy...grab my wellies
And for luck, three extra frocks.

Now there's really nothing for it
Drag down suitcase number four,
Have to lie on lid to shut it
(Technique learned from three before!)

Now I'm feeling much more happy
Though regret one thing I'll lack;
But resigned! There's no solution;
My Tiara won't flat pack!

Are We Nearly There, Mum?

'Are we nearly there, mum?
When will we arrive?'
Uttered by my offspring
As *we pull out of our drive...*

I tell them, 'It's ten seconds down
And four more hours to go.'
The car erupts with groaning
And exaggerated woe!

And then begins the old routine;
'I'm bored' or 'I feel sick'
With intermittent action
Of the odd punch, scream or kick.

Requests for ice-cream, drinks, the loo,
They irritate me rather,
Not least because a lot of them
Are coming from *their Father!*

And then of course when we get lost
Things do tense up a tad;
And back seat violence can't compare
With front seat Mum v Dad!

At least the 'How long?' routine
Has stopped now, to be fair,
But then they have been busy
Ripping out each other's hair.

Are limbs now being *broken*,
Or just severely bruised?
But hell, it's their choice how they opt
To keep themselves amused!

'Why don't you look for V reg cars?'
The desperate mother cries,
A quick glance in rear mirror shows
Two sets of rolling eyes!

Two urgent questions cross my mind
As I attempt to drive;
'Are we nearly there yet?
And WHEN WILL WE ARRIVE?'

Iron Lady

We set off on our holiday
We've not gone very far,
When all at once... a ghastly thought;
I shriek, 'Please stop the car!'

The family won't like this news
And he'll look put upon
When I announce, 'We must go back
I've left the iron on!'

My husband stays quite taciturn
Just wears a 'No Way' scowl.
'So you'd just let our home burn down
Without a thought?' I howl.

A violent argument ensues
I plead and his teeth gnash.
(I visualise the fire brigade
Now sifting through the ash.)

But luckily I win the day
We turn back. I hiss, '*Faster!*'
Just hoping we get there in time
To limit the disaster.

He growls, 'I know the iron's off
And so, deep down, do you!
REMEMBER LAST YEAR WITH THE GRILL?
I'm getting déjà vu!'

Arriving home in record time
My fears somewhat allayed;
No sign of any belching smoke
Nor of the fire brigade.

But we are not out of the woods
And I won't speak too soon!
(There might be an inferno
Raging in the breakfast room.)

Though heart a little less in mouth
I enter cautiously,
But I've mixed feeling when I see
What lies in store for me.

The iron's safely on a shelf,
Unplugged it would appear.
I wonder how HE'LL take this news...
Just like a man...I fear!

Mile-High Grub

When travelling by plane
You'll always find me quite subdued;
It's not my fear of flying though
More dread of airline food!
As time goes by, my palms will sweat
My anguish will be real;
It's not, 'Will this plane crash?'
But, 'Will I get a decent meal?'

Let's start off with the packaging
And first cause to complain;
You need *a ruddy saw* to cut
Through all that cellophane!
The struggle has left many meals
Upturned upon one's lap.
NB When faced with *solid* food
The cutlery will snap!

Next, staring with confusion
At a most suspicious dish,
You *can't* make out the contents!
Is it chicken, cheese or fish?
The thing that is disturbing
Is that fifteen minutes on
You're really none the wiser
Even when the whole lot's gone.

The bread is polystyrene-based
The 'French' cheese tastes like soap,
But the mint is looking hopeful!
Decent coffee? Not a hope!
And once the meal is over
Don't expect to feel replete;
Just remember for the future
Before flying, always eat!

Maybe Concorde is quite different
From economy I've seen
That the higher up you get you find
The less haute the cuisine.

It's the Way They Tell It

In the brochure the hotel seemed splendid
'Cross one road to the beautiful bay'
Not a hint or suggestion
That the one road in question
Was a brand new six-lane motorway.

'From the bedrooms the views are quite stunning'
(It's a phrase that reads so well on paper)
Very true, I've no doubt
Had they not been blocked out
By a newly-constructed skyscraper.

As we love to cool off in the water
When we read of the pool we were thrilled,
But our hopes of a swim
Were exceedingly slim
For the big concrete hole was not filled.

'The hotel is quaint' sounded charming
But the sub-text is easily missed
For their meaning of quaint
Means the plumbing just ain't
Quite as modern as one might have wished.

Now an accurate idea of distance
Is a concept you somehow expect;
'Town Centre – short walk'
Was just brochure-esque talk
And that three-hour round trip left us wrecked.

Well they said that '*The night life is lively*'
And it was in its own special way;
What a novel approach
To include a cockroach
In the nightly 'ensuite cabaret'.

Since the dream that we bought was a nightmare
We decided to cut our stay short;
But can't wait till we show
Our six-hour video
Of our holiday...next month IN COURT!

A Suitable Bay

I marvel at this horseshoe bay
The shady palms, the soft white sand
And in my hammock gently sway
Exotic cocktail in one hand.

And now a local girl strolls by
A basket carried on her hip
Papayas, mangoes catch my eye;
A snack before I take a dip.

Folk busy barbecuing lunch
Now shout 'Be ready in a trice!'
And as I laze I have a hunch
That this could well be paradise.

And suddenly I'm wide awake
'I want a lolly' in my ear.
What's this? There must be some mistake!
I should be there, but I am here!

And gradually the feeling grows
That some small detail is not right;
Although there's sand between my toes
The sea – alas – nowhere in sight.

It seems I'm not quite on *that bay*
As I had hoped, but to be fair
There is a lot that one can say
In praise of Weston Super Mare!

Bronze-Age Blues

Devotees of the sun... BEWARE!
Or you'll acquire quite soon
A leather finish to your bod
And face that's like a prune.

Though you've been told a thousand times
You do not seem to learn
That mental sun-block is for fools;
So DON'T go for the burn.

If you *must* lie out in the sun,
At least control your fate,
Protect yourself with sun-tan cream
And get your factors straight.

No, let's not beat about the bush,
For once burnt to a crisp
The lobster-look-alikes will find
Their health might be at risk.

But there is further good advice
And you'd be wise to take it;
If you are going for bronze or gold
The best way is to fake it!

Our love affair with *le soleil*
Must sadly be reviewed;
These days, sun doesn't play a part
In the tanning of the shrewd.

Don't Tent Me

I'd love to be an outdoor type
But it is not my style.
Just whisper tent-peg in my ear
And I will run a mile.

Why others opt for camping
Is quite a mystery;
To be 'at one' with nature
Is *far* too close for me.

Those campers lead a healthy life
Which is to be admired.
But sanitation truth to tell
Leaves much to be desired.

I know my limitations
And it has come to pass
I like to reach a flushing loo
Without contact with grass.

Those campers rise at daybreak
To see a new day dawning,
But who wants mud and cows and fields
So early in the morning?

Those campers sit around a fire
But sadly never learn
That camp-fire food, it never cooks
Just goes straight for the burn!

As one who once embraced the life
I say this with deep feeling;
Damp sleeping bags and rampant cramp
Are just not that appealing.

So with each year that passes
On this I am hell bent;
To keep well clear of canvas
Will be my firm in-tent!

All for Juan... and Juan for All

Young Pépé is swarthy and handsome
He's also a very smooth talker;
Sweet nothings are spoken
And hearts will get broken
Under star-studded skies of Majorca.

Beware girls! Don't fall for that charmer
For your romance may well end in grief;
Yes, that gorgeous young Juan
Is just out for some fun
Which will end when you leave Tenerife.

So, you footloose young ladies... be careful
For your recklessness may takes its toll;
Don't let down all defences
Don't lose grip of your senses
Don't go mad on the Costa del Sol.

Far from home, watch this lass lose her heart to
One she'd normally think was beneath her.
But with hot sun you'll find
Love is horribly blind
Even creeps can look good in Ibiza.

Oh the pain when that fortnight is over,
And the memories... so bittersweet.
So you fell for Miguel;
I did warn you. Oh well.
Next year take my advice and try Crete.

So Sad the Thong

To you, thong-wearers of the world
I hate to be unkind.
But are you really sure you know
What you look like
From behind?

Home Sweet Home

In Praise of the Humble Fish Finger

A tribute to Fish Fingers
Is very overdue,
Without them I'd be truly stumped
At tea time, wouldn't you?

Enjoyed whenever eaten,
Prepared with ease (Thank God!)
Though battered, can't be beaten...
Here's looking at you, Cod!

What Time is Supper
(or *What a Difference a Day Makes*)

Pre onset of PMT...

'It's nearly ready, Darling.
I'll quickly test the meat,
Just pour yourself a glass of wine,
Relax...put up your feet.
Just garnishing the hors d'hoeuvres
And whipping up the cream,
Yes, Darling it's three courses
And I'm talking haute cuisine!
Yes ready in a jiff, dear,
Sit down and then I'll serve
It's all your favourite dishes
And no more than you deserve.'

...Onset of PMT.

'Oh yes, good question sunshine!
Well I've got news for you,
The answer is quite simply
That I haven't got a clue,
And in case you hadn't noticed
(I scream, brandishing a mallet)
I've better things to do right now
Than titillate your palate.'
And just to make my meaning clear,
Hurl baked bean tin from shelf,
With tonight's serving suggestion
'Heat them up your bloody self!'

This Cheating Art

Dear Spouse, I wish I had the flair
To cook meals to impress.
But my attempts just don't compare
To those from M and S.
Yet think of all the time I save
In cooking every day;
Just pierce that film and microwave
Then bin the tinfoil tray!
But it is with a heavy heart
I justify this habit;
Yes, lacking culinary art
A chance to cheat...I'll grab it!
And though I see no other way
On this thought I do brood,
Ours is, I'm mortified to say,
A marriage of convenience food!

Happy Shopper

Rather rashly, ask spouse to go shopping.
Write a list out, so he won't forget.
But of course he insists
He has no need for lists
Something *one* of us will soon regret.

When he turns up a good few hours later
I notice, when we start unpacking
He's scored really high
On the old 'impulse buy'
But the staples are, sadly, all lacking.

I try to look grateful, excited
Hide my horror, keep smiling instead.
'Kiwi chutney mmm...fine,
Lobster bisque.... Yes divine
But please tell me that you bought sliced bread.'

He produces an olive ciabbata
'Looks fun, eh?' Well I have a hunch
That conservative son
Won't find Dad's choice *such* fun
With Nutella...in his school packed lunch.

Though the Duck terrine does look quite tasty
To be brutally honest I wish
That he'd bought the pâté
In a less costly way
i.e. not in large pottery dish.

And although I'm a fan of papaya
Today it was not a wise buy;
For a tropical fruit
Is no real substitute
When you're planning to make apple pie.

When I finally spot the six quails eggs
My frustration is too great to hide;
'How the hell can I make
This lot into a cake
Let alone fit a soldier inside?'

Though in some ways I like spouse's choices
And his buys have exotic appeal
They are no help to one
Who, when all said and done,
Needs the wherewithal for a square meal.

Now he's speaking, 'You find shopping boring...
I don't get it, I find it such fun!'
He is smiling as he
Nibbles *foie gras* and brie
While I silently reach for my gun.

All Washed Up

When he became my husband
And I became his wife,
I hoped he'd do the washing up
And save me endless strife.

But disappointment lay in store
A tale that oft unfolds...
In truth, it was yours truly
Who wore those Marigolds!

I thought this was a mite unfair,
And things came to a head;
'I'd like help with the washing up...
And there's the sink!' I said.

He didn't shirk the issue
I'll hand it to the man;
'I can't do washing up,' said he,
'But I know something that can!'

Then enter one dishwasher
Oh joy, oh ecstasy!
I binned my rubber gloves that day
With wild, unbridled glee.

We bonded firmly from the first
We've been close ever since,
That cycle's music to my ears
First wash to final rinse.

Domestic bliss reigns in our home
And perfect harmony
With our eternal triangle...
Dishwasher, spouse and me!

And I Say to Myself ...
What A Wonderful Weld

When you went in for DIY
I gave you my support,
And out of ten
The marks I gave
Were generous at NOUGHT.

What you achieved left me nonplussed
Though I tried hard to hide it,
But *home improvement*
To be frank
Is NOT how I'd describe it.

Yes, though it was a gift from me
That brand new Black and Decker,
In your hands
Has turned out to be
A positive home *wrecker*.

Not just *our* home of course, my sweet
With no effort at all,
You drilled
A nice new opening
Right through a party wall!

Our neighbours took it very well
Stayed calm. In fact I'd say
It rendered them
Quite speechless.
The court case is next May.

You may think me ungrateful;
A wife who just complains
But then,who laid
The patio
And blocked up all the drains?

Who said the bracket you put up
Would never need re-mounting?
You've welded it
Back in to place
Nine times now (But who's counting?)

And while I hate to rush you
The bathroom's still not done,
You promised it
Would be in use
Before the millennium.

And though I know you do your best
Well darling as I speak,
The pipe that you
Have just plumbed in
Has sprung a nasty leak.

And as I watch my toiletries
Slide slowly off the shelf,
What can I say
But dearest
Please
DON'T DO IT YOURSELF!

It's Curtains for You

Oh why do men groan or start yawning,
Roll their eyes, shrug their shoulders or wince
When you ask for their views
On which curtains to choose
Why are males so allergic to chintz?

And why do they think it's *our* problem
And consider us terrible nags
And glaze over or frown
When we're pinning them down
On their preference for flounces or swags?

Do they merely consider such questions
As just boring, irrelevant hassle?
They'll treat with derision
The crucial decision
Concerning the tie-back or tassel.

A scene that's frustrating and thankless.
The refurbishing female oft finds
That one thing's for certain
Men just won't choose curtains
Or do gentlemen just prefer blinds?

Anyone who had a Hearth

If you possess an open fire
You'll know that special thrill
Of lighting your first autumn fire
Once evenings grow quite chill.

You'll also know the minus points;
The sudden downward gust
Which gives your cosy sitting room
A coating of *thick dust!*

You will recall the summer months
When there is no fire burning
And visits from our 'feathered friends'
Who've taken a wrong turning.

But pros do far outweigh the cons
A fireside can't be beat;
And whingers should steer clear of grates
If they can't take the heat!

While swirling smoke, thick tar and dust
Can make the 'house-proud' weep;
I take it philosophically.
It's sooty...so I sweep!

The Pile-High Club

You find my desk a shocking mess
And I am not surprised,
But friend, appearances deceive;
It's highly organised!
Those papers stacked up over there
Well that's my 'Pending Tray'
(My euphemism for the phrase
'May sort it out...some day!')

You'll no doubt think my 'Action' pile
Suggests one word; Confusion!
But please do take my word for it;
You've reached the wrong conclusion.
This seemingly chaotic stash
Belies a strategy
Of systematic filing
That's known only to me.

And finally, this heap of stuff
Or 'Big Pile Number 3'
Needs to be filed...in other piles!
Its called miscellany.
There's order in this chaos
Things aren't as they appear.
But no one else can tell I've got
Procedures in place here.

And now you must be wondering
Where's the technology?
Although it's out of sight I do
Possess great gadgetry.
Beneath this highly ordered mass
Are aids that I hold dear,
My PC, printer, fax and phone
Are... *somewhere under here.*

Absolute Beginner

They say don't ask your husband
To teach you how to drive,
The same goes for computers
For the marriage to survive!
'I'll only tell you once,' says he,
'So please, do pay attention!'
(*That's just the type of comment*
To cause marital-type tension).
Why does he lose his bottle
And seem so put upon
When asked, 'Please dearest, *one last time...*
How do I switch it on?'

What drama! I've lost half my work!
I'm desperately dismayed.
But 'Him Indoors' will sort me out;
My fears will be allayed.
And then he strikes a chilling note
His words fills me with terror;
'You didn't save! It's all *your* fault!
Don't blame computer error!'
But there's no way that I'll concede
I'm wrong and he is right;
So I yell back, 'I BLOODY WILL!'
(My bark's worse than my byte)

Growing Old Disgracefully

Optical Delusion

Those microwave instructions
Have been printed far too small.
I squint, I hold them near and far.
Can't make them out at all.

Spouse says that I need glasses.
I treat this with derision.
It's such a daft suggestion for
Someone with perfect vision.

Feeling Groovy

New specs and my reflection
Is thoroughly inspected.
Dismayed to find 'flaws' hitherto
Completely undetected.

Myopic, how was I to know
The mirror told me lies
And kept me from developments
Like CRATERS round my eyes!

Rush straight down to cosmetic store
I need some help and quick!
Some cream will surely smooth me out
If slapped on mega thick.

Appealing to the sales girl
·For an instant remedy
Her look of pity says it all;
There's not much hope for me.

She tries hard to be tactful
But she's going for home truths;
'Those aren't just fine lines, Madam,
They're more like – well – DEEP GROOVES!'

Quite clear that I am too far gone
For anti-ageing cream
She offers me a product
That *covers up* a dream!

Enriched with luscious lipisomes
But sadly here's the rub;
Only the wealthy need apply
It's fifty quid a tub!

I bid farewell to help from hell
Resisting urge to kill her.
And ponder facial benefits
Of good old POLYFILLER!

Two Sleepy People

What happened to the ravers
Who 'out-partied' all their friends,
Who disco-danced till dawn
And burnt the candle at both ends?

We did not care two hoots for sleep,
A few hours did us fine,
We never thought, 'We're doing well...
We're still awake at nine!'

We never yawned when friends stayed late
Our eye-lids never drooped.
And we were never heard to say,
'I'm off to bed, I'm pooped.'

Though we recall the way we were
We now accept our fate,
We know that it's called 'middle age'
We really can't do 'late'.

And nowadays those yawns flow free
We don't fight drooping lids,
Too well aware we hit the sack
Most nights before the kids.

To simplify how life is now
And how it was back then,
It's much less, 'Rock around the Clock'
And much more, 'Snooze at Ten'.

State of the Archaic

Embracing new technology
Is my idea of hell
I feel too old to learn new tricks
(They hurt my brain as well).

But thankfully my toddler
Is really in the know;
He sends my e-mails off for me
And sets the video.

Such a Perfect Dye

My passing into middle age
Is plain for all to see;
My hair is slowly turning
From grey...to MAHOGANY!

In the Neck of Time

Some bits of me have not aged well
As often is the way;
My neck has rather let me down...
It gives the game away!

That tell-tale scrawny sagginess
Now cannot be ignored
*(Though luckily my double chins
Keep some of it obscured!)*

What was once smooth and oh so sleek
Has sadly gone to seed,
And times I stick my neck out
Are very rare indeed.

And though I've fought decrepitude
In a multitude of ways
I must concede my prolapsed jowls
Have both seen better days.

So much for all those costly creams
Applied with upward strokes,
When faced with rampant rumpling
They just can't hack it, folks.

So I avoid décolletées
And never wear a V
The scoop and off-the-shoulder too
For me are history.

Instead I sport a polo neck
A scarf can help as well
(*When warmer weather comes it's tough...*
And on the beach... IT'S HELL!)

The fight to halt time's ravages
Is one we cannot win
And I must just accept my lot...
Knackered Neck
And Crêpe de Chin!

Food for Thought

There was a time not long ago
That I can still recall
When my kitchen ran like clockwork
And my eye stayed on the ball.

These days I'm more forgetful
Just a symptom of my age;
I sometimes lose the plot
Upon the gastronomic stage.

Now the '*Somewhat-Absent-Minded*
School of Cuisine' has in store
All the vegetables... *al dente*
And the joint... completely raw!

And later when the bird is done
I note, on close inspection,
The giblets *in their plastic bag*
Have been cooked to perfection!

I know my once high standards
Have taken quite a tumble
What with custard on lasagne
And a bechamel on the crumble!

Oh ghastly gastronomic gaffes;
Even Delia can't save me...
But life's full of surprises
When you've one foot in the gravy!

Waking Up is Hard to Do

Time was when I would leap from bed
Just as the day was dawning
I'd stretch, breathe deeply, greet the day
With a most robust, 'Good morning.'

I'd exercise those nimble limbs
Most energetically
Before a most invigorating
Cup of herbal tea.

But many years have passed since then.
And as can now be seen
There have been *subtle* changes
In the early morn regime.

These days there's not much leaping
(Due to *risk of injury!*)
My style's more *casual stagger*
I move...but gingerly.

These days recharging batteries
Takes more than herbal tea;
The drink's now strong black coffee
Taken intravenously.

And what of all that exercise?
IT'S OUT! For strictly speaking
I'm trying hard to minimise
The sound of chronic creaking!

Growing Old Disgracefully
(or *Tactful Tips for the Oldest Raver in Town*)

Dear friend before your daughter's 18th party
Some things a chap *your age* might like to know;
It's most unwise to imitate Mick Jagger
Likewise to 'air-guitar' to Status Quo!
You know that 'little dance' you've done for decades
Where you 'Travolta' right across the floor?
I think it's only fair that I should tell you
That people just don't do that any more.
PLEASE do not ask for 'Hey Ho Silver Lining'
Or anything that's sung by Picketty Witch
And do not do your Elvis Presley routine
You know it always gives you such a stitch.
Of course you must enjoy this special evening,
We'd hate to cramp your style in any way
But feel perhaps the time has come to tell you
'IT'S TIME TO PUT THOSE TIGER FEET AWAY'.

Ode to a Twenty-One-Year-Old

Twenty-one
Twenty-one!
Life has only just begun.

Unfettered. Fearless, full of hope
The world's your oyster
Full of scope.

So much to do, to learn, to see.
Go!
Seize each opportunity!

(And if all this seems a trifle zealous
It's to hide the fact that I'm so jealous!)

Generation Gaffe

What is the nation coming to?
Well something should be done;
What's happened to policemen?
They all look far too young.
I spot them bravely fighting crime
With danger ever near,
I want to say, 'Hey sonny
Does your mother know you're here?'

And then those junior doctors
They hate it as a rule
When I look them up and down and say,
'Shouldn't you be at school?'
I search for reassurance
To put my fears aside,
'Are you *sure* you've got A-levels?
Are you *really* qualified?'

Perhaps some think it's no big deal
But it worries me a tad
That my child's personal tutor
Seems no more than a lad.
What wisdom can this boy possess?
What knowledge? I despair;
He's just out of short trousers
And has no facial hair.

I voice these observations
It's normal I am told.
Those chaps are just as they should be
It's just me who's getting old.

The Wrong Trousers
(Not to Mention Shoes and Knickers)

I think the 'leggings look' is now behind me
And jeans with lycra no more to my taste.
My needs have changed, in middle age you'll find me
Clad in a *looser* cut (with comfort waist).
As far as footwear goes, I've shrunk two inches
It's goodbye to the old stiletto heel,
I've cast aside the sexy shoe that pinches;
Hush Puppies frankly have much more appeal.
As for my knicker drawer – I've been spring-cleaning;
All skimpy garments have been laid to rest
My preference for lingerie now leaning
Towards thermal long-johns (with a matching vest)
So farewell trendy gear and Janet Reager
It's hello Damart and smart tweeds from Jaeger.

Thin Ice

Spouse meant it as a compliment
But women can be fickle;
'*How dare you call me well-preserved,
I'm not a ruddy* PICKLE'.

And then he really went too far
I felt the urge to thump him
I said, 'I'm feeling fat and old'
He said, 'CHINS UP, MY DUMPLING'.

Swings and Roundabouts

Some people faced with wrinkling
Will simply go to pieces
But wisdom and maturity
Outweigh my mid-life creases.

If you have enjoyed this book, now read Judy Rose's first title
A Fridge Over Troubled Water, £5.99 + £1.00 postage

HOW TO ORDER

BY TELEPHONE   Please call between 9.30 am and 5.30 pm Monday to Friday
on 01608 652012 / 652025

BY FAX   Please complete the form below and fax to us on 01608 652125

BY POST   Please complete this form and post to: The Windrush Press, Little
Window, High Street, Moreton-in-Marsh, Gloucestershire, GL56 0LL

OR VISIT OUR WEBSITE   www.windrushpress.com

NAME & ADDRESS (BLOCK CAPITALS PLEASE)

Name . . . .

Address . . . .

. . . .

Postcode . . . .

I enclose a cheque for £   made payable to The Windrush Press

Or, please debit my Mastercard/Visa/American Express/Switch
Card Details
Number

Expiry Date   Issue Number (Switch only)

Signature